10 YEAR C

MW00876210

I am 10 and Amazing

Inspiring True Stories of Courage, Self-Esteem, Self-Love, and self-Confidence

Paula Collins

© Copyright 2022 - Paula Collins

www.paulacollins.online

paula.collins@paulacollins.online

It is not legal to reproduce, duplicate, or transmit any part of this document in either electronic means or in printed format. Recording of this publication is strictly prohibited and any storage of this document is not al owed unless with written permission from the publisher except for the use of brief quotations in a book review.

This book is a work of fiction. Any resemblance to persons, living or dead, or places, events or locations is purely coincidental.

Contents

Introduction

Hello! Do you realize how amazing you are?

You are exceptional. You are completely unique. Always remember that! You are the only you there is in the entire world, and that's out of billions of people!

The world has many big and small hurdles in store for you. Sometimes you might think that you can't make it. You might get very scared or doubt yourself. However, I want to tell you a secret. Everybody feels like this from time to time! Even adults.

In this Inspiring Stories book, you will meet other amazing girls. These girls overcome their fears, show great inner strength, and reveal their bravery.

Of course, you can show all these qualities too, but you must start believing in yourself. That is exactly what this book will help you learn to do.

You can shine your light in your corner of the world

and bring that light to other people when you let go of fear and keep learning lessons. When you believe in yourself, you can accomplish anything. You are an Amazing girl.

I wish Upon a Shooting Star

Have you ever had a furry friend at home? Did they ever feel unwell and need to see a vet? Here's a story about a girl who really loved and wished the best for her little kitten.

Aurora fell in love with the cat when she met her and named her Fluffball. She didn't care that she wasn't perfect, as her ears were not both pointed, but rather one was folded over as if it had fallen. It was a small deformity, but Aurora didn't care. Although Fluffball looked different, Aurora thought she was the prettiest kitten. She was probably abandoned for being different, so she deserved a home. From that scared, hungry, and cold day, she became a part of the family.

Aurora knew everyone would see Fluffball just like any other cat. She was just a regular kitty who loved to play.

Fluffball had a thing for yarn balls, unraveling them whenever she found one, and she did the same with toilet paper! She sometimes used the living room furniture to sharpen her claws, but after getting her a scratching post, she stopped doing that.

They showed Fluffball how to use a litter box they placed on the balcony. Most of the time, she was either playful or snoozing. When she was up, she loved to play around. And when she got tired, she'd just drift off to sleep, lying on her back with her little paws sticking out.

Aurora built her a tunnel with cardboard boxes that went along the entire living room, and she stood on the other side, talking to her through the hole.

"Come, Fluffball, I'm waiting for you here. Come on,

you can pass there; I'll look after you."

Fluffball looked curious, sniffing the tunnel to figure out what it was. After a moment, she decided to trust Aurora and began to carefully walk through, checking out every part of this new space. Aurora cheered her on gently, urging her to keep going. And when Fluffball finally made it to the other side, Aurora gave her a big hug and listened to her happy purrs.

Next, Aurora came up with a fun game. She tossed a ball into one end of the tunnel. Fluffball darted after it like a soccer player, quickly emerging on the other side with the ball. Soon, she was racing back and forth through the tunnel, looking so happy with her new game. They both had a blast!

One day, Fluffball wasn't her usual playful self. Instead of running around and playing, she looked really tired. Her nose was dry and something about her face seemed off. Aurora's family thought maybe she ate something bad, especially when they noticed her tummy looked bigger the next day. Seeing Fluffball looking like she needed help, Aurora's dad said, "I think we need to take Fluffball to the vet. She doesn't look well and might need a doctor's care."

Aurora felt a knot in her stomach. Why was Fluffball

sick? The idea scared her. Her dad quickly prepared to take Fluffball to the vet. Aurora noticed him talking with her mom, both looking concerned.

Later, after visiting the animal hospital, Aurora and her parents left with heavy hearts. They had to leave Fluffball there for some tests to figure out what was wrong.

When they got home, her mother said, "Think good thoughts, daughter, put all your positive thoughts in motion, so Fluffball gets better; she will surely do so."

"We will go out to the garden tonight and do something that will work." Aurora didn't understand anything, but she said yes.

"What are we going to do?" asked Aurora, who didn't understand what her mother was talking about.

"We will ask a star for Fluffball's health."

That night, they went out to the garden and lay on the soft grass, looking up at the twinkling stars. Mom whispered, "Close your eyes, Aurora. Wish with all your heart for Fluffball to get better and come home. Imagine her playing and maybe scratching the furniture just a tiny bit. Wish for her to be happy and healthy."

"Okay," said Aurora.

" We must keep hoping, so they have much power and come true; you will see how it works."

"I'm doing it; I'm already doing it," said Aurora.

The next morning, as Aurora brushed her hair, an eyelash fell. She gently picked it up and made a wish before blowing it away. She felt that it was a good sign. Later, they walked by a park with a shimmering fountain. Stopping for a moment, they took out some coins and made wishes for Fluffball as they tossed them into the water.

That night, they took out a piece of cake and placed a candle on top. They sang "Happy Birthday", even if it wasn't anyone's birthday. They just wanted to make another wish for Fluffball. After the song, Aurora closed her eyes tightly, made her wish, and blew out the candle. They wanted to try every possible way to send positive vibes to Fluffball. But in the end, they knew they had to trust the doctors to help her.

Her dad came home with an update about Fluffball. The vet said that she was still not feeling well, and they were doing their best to help her. He suggested that they could visit Fluffball to spend some time with her. Kneeling down to Aurora's level, he gently explained that their little kitty was quite ill and needed a lot of strength.

"I know you've been wishing really hard for Fluffball to get better. And I believe all your positive wishes helped. You know what? Fluffball was going to have kittens. Even though she had a tough time before she came to us, something magical happened. However..."

Her dad gently pulled out a tiny kitten from a little bag. The kitten looked so much like Fluffball, only smaller and a boy. Its cute little paws and soft meow melted Aurora's heart right away.

"What do you think we should name him?" her dad asked, noticing Aurora's big smile. "How about 'Bowl'? It's like 'ball' but sounds a bit more boyish," Aurora suggested. "I love it," her father agreed. That night, after tucking Bowl into a cozy bed and giving him lots of cuddles, Aurora gazed out at the starry sky. "Fluffball," she whispered, "I promise to take the best care of your little one." And who says wishes don't come true?

Losing a pet can hurt, but like us, they have their own journeys. So, cherish every moment you have with your furry friends.

Spark

Do you like animals? Did you know dogs can join fun contests and win because of their tricks and training? This story is about a girl who worked really hard and, with kindness and training, got the dog she always dreamed of.

When Mila was a little girl, she fell in love with dogs. One day, she met a beautiful dog and felt a special bond. She just knew she would always love it. Excited, she began reading many books about dogs from the library, learning about how to care for them and train them."

She discovered a book about training dogs to do special tricks and poses, especially for dog shows. These dogs could walk through tiny tunnels, hop over little hurdles, and even stand on their hind legs! It was funny because they sometimes acted more like people than dogs.

She watched some videos online and saw how amazing dog training was. There were simple tricks like sitting and fetching, and super cool ones like helping find lost people or even knowing if someone was sick. Mila loved everything about it, so she asked her dad if she could take classes to become a dog trainer. Guess what? He said yes!"

Before long, Mila was teaching tricks to their family dog. She also met other kids who loved training dogs just as much as she did. Her love for everything about dogs kept growing and growing!

After many months of hard work and learning, Mila had a big wish. She wanted a dog of her own. Sure, there was Tino, the old family dog, but he had been with her dad for a very long time. Mila loved Tino, but she wanted a younger dog she could train. Tino was more her dad's buddy. She had been good, finishing her schoolwork and being nice to everyone. So, one day, she asked her dad if she could get her own dog. He smiled and said, 'If you find the right one, sure!

At first, Mila thought about buying a dog. But then she remembered hearing that it's better to adopt because there are so many dogs in shelters who need homes. So, she asked her mom to visit some shelters. She hoped to find a young, energetic dog that was excited to learn new things.

On a sunny Saturday morning, Mila and her mom visited several dog shelters. Every time they met a dog, Mila wished she could take them all home because they looked so eager to be with her. But she was searching for a special dog to train for shows. Finally, someone told them about a dog in another shelter that might be just right. If they hurried, they might be able to adopt it that day.

In the car, Mila was bubbling with excitement. Her mom quickly typed the shelter's address into the GPS. When they got there, Mila explained what kind of dog she was hoping to find. She didn't need a fancy purebred dog, but she did want one that would be good for training. Some dogs, she knew, were a bit stubborn and might be trickier to teach.

At the shelter, a kind woman led them through many doors until they reached a big room. "I hope you like him," she said, pointing inside. There was a thin black dog with unique orange spots on his back. Mila's heart raced with excitement. The dog looked at them carefully, wagging his tail slowly. But then, he suddenly stopped wagging and growled a little.

The woman explained, "Poor thing was treated badly by some mean people. That's why he's a bit scared. But with some love and patience, he'll be okay.

"What's his name?" Mila asked.

"We don't know his name; we call him Spark. He seems to understand his name because when we say it, he looks at us."

"Spark," Mila said softly, calling him by his new name. The dog's ears perked up a bit when he heard her. The woman gave her some dog food, and she put it in her hand. The dog lifted his nose and approached slowly, looking at Mila's and her mother's faces. He moved his head a bit, and everyone looked at each other momentarily. Then, he started eating from her hand, still a bit tense.

He took another bite when he finished eating what was in his mouth. Mila studied him, and she knew she had found the perfect dog. He was the most beautiful dog she had ever seen. What could be an ugly and aggressive dog for others was the best, unique dog for her that would leave a mark wherever he went.

Mila said, "I want him." Spark seemed a bit scared at first, but when Mila gently petted him, he relaxed. She took him home and they became the best of friends. Mila taught Spark all the cool tricks she had learned. Spark was a quick learner, and soon he was winning awards at dog shows. Everyone wanted to see Mila and her amazing dog Spark.

Sometime later, many ribbons and medals adorned the walls of their home. Their effort had paid off.

Persistence, continuous learning, and doing good things yield great results for people and animals.

A Great Mother

Have you ever felt a little shy because of something your mom did? Do you like helping people? This is the tale of a mom and her daughter having a memorable day at a place for elderly folks.

Carrie stared at her mom, who was grinning from ear to ear. Dressed in a huge orange bunny costume with big floppy ears, she looked like one of those characters you see outside stores. And there she stood, holding a wicker basket.

Carrie was shocked! She thought being her age was already tricky, but seeing her mom dressed like that made it even crazier. She tried to convince her mom to let her stay home. "I have chores," Carrie said. "And I think I caught a bad flu!" But no matter what she said, they were going.

They went to the place where her mom would wear the bunny suit. As they entered, a lot of people were laughing and pointing at the bunny. Carrie felt so embarrassed! She wished she could just disappear. She even thought of running out of there.

"Hello, bunny," said one of the gentlemen in the room.

"Do you know who's inside that costume?" asked a grandma.

"No idea, I don't know who it is," said Carrie.

Everyone in the room started laughing as they watched the bunny doing many things. They were in line waiting for the bunny to say something with that fun and charisma that it had. Some had walkers in their hands and smiled as if they were children, with those wrinkled, toothless mouths, but the sweetest of all.

Carrie's mother explained to her that, in many cases, there were special people there. Now that they were older, they needed medical attention for various reasons. They all lived there, and Carrie thought they were grandparents who had been forgotten, but her mother told her that not all of them. Some visited them, others had never had children, and others were indeed forgotten because their children had gone to another country.

A lady approached Carrie; she seemed to be the one coordinating that center and gave her some flowers, telling her to give one to each senior.

Carrie thought back to last year when she had dressed up as a squirrel and had so much fun playing with everyone. But now, she felt different, like she was too old for dress-up. Still, she did as she was told and began giving out flowers to all the elderly people. They all smiled and thanked her warmly.

Many other kids, about Carrie's age, were there too. Some had already handed out their flowers. It seemed like a tradition that everyone followed. Without questioning, they all accepted the flowers with joy. "Why are they giving out flowers? Silly folks," grumbled an old man, looking around with a frown.

He was a man who sometimes forgot things because of a condition he had. This made him a bit grumpy at times. The people at the center said he was mostly kind, but they also said it was best not to be alone with him.

Carrie and the man became friends. Sometimes, he'd give her a candy or gently pat her head when she walked by, always smiling kindly. He would often call her "Candy." Her mom told her that he had a daughter named Candy a long time ago. Even though Candy was now grown up, because of his condition, he sometimes got a little mixed up.

Everyone was busy with their activities, preparing for that moment they were waiting for. The small number where Carrie's mother brightened up their day.

"Want to play?" a kid asked Carrie.

"Maybe in a bit," she replied, her eyes still on her mom in the rabbit suit.

Soon, the room grew quiet, and the lights dimmed. It was time for the show!

"Do you know who's in the rabbit costume?" someone whispered to Carrie. "Kind of..." she answered shyly.

"You're doing great here!" the person smiled, giving her more flowers to share.

Carrie rolled her eyes; she thought she was in a great dilemma with many rules and things to do. She started handing out the flowers to other people again. Everyone talked about that flower girl and how dedicated she was.

"She's such a kind girl," someone commented, "but she should be playing with kids her own age." Carrie looked around. Everywhere she saw were warm, loving faces of the elderly. Their smiles were genuine, and they seemed happy to see her. She returned their smiles and approached a very old lady with a walker. "How are you feeling?" she asked. "As spry as a 96-year-old can be!" the old lady chuckled.

Carrie gave flowers to all the elderly people in the room. Some kids watched quietly, their eyes full of wonder. Then, a kind lady in charge came over and gave Carrie a warm, comforting hug.

"My mom was in a nursing home for years; I wish she had sweet girls like you and a mother like yours. They brighten up the lives of these elderly people."

Carrie's mother began to jump and continue with her number while thanking everyone for coming.

Something inside Carrie sparked. She realized she was lucky and giving something to people who wanted it, so with pride, she said out loud, " Every year, my mother and I come here to serve."

Everyone started applauding with big smiles.

A boy exclaimed, "Wow, my mom would never dress up like that! Your mom is so cool." He smiled, a hint of envy in his eyes, and walked away. Many other kids also shared nice things about their moms, but Carrie's mom surely stood out that day.

The rabbit mom spoke about everything they did in that place. About programs not only for the elderly but also for children and adults. That everyone could be volunteers and even go after school. The grandparents applauded happily.

That day Carrie realized that helping others was great and that her mother had some angel in her for giving herself to help people who weren't her family but needed a hand.

Carrie knew that she had a bunch of grandparents in that house because they saw her as a granddaughter.

Never feel ashamed of your mother, even less so when she does a good deed. And when you can, give to those in need.

Discovering New Cultures

Have you ever imagined how many kilometers around the world is? Millions? How do you think they live? Do you think they are like you or do their own things? This story shows how every culture is different and has its own ways of living.

Since Aura had arrived in that new country after traveling many hours on a plane where she felt like she had circled the planet 8 times, they finally landed.

She had already seen people everywhere, who spoke a little differently than her, who had a different way of being, the clothes, their faces, the way they even walked. She knew she was not at home, that it was a different culture.

Already at her cousins' house, where she had gone to spend some time, at her uncle's house, she had dinner placed in front of her; it was a plate with many vegetables on top, piled high. Aura looked at them with fear.

Her cousin was next to her and looked at her strangely.

"What is this, Charlie?" She asked her cousin.

"Food."

"Yes, but I haven't seen it, what is the yellow thing?" She asked again.

"They are all vegetables, and if you try them, you will like them. We eat them a lot here."

Charlie couldn't stop looking at her with amusement.

" Since I came to this place, everything has been so... strange," Aura said.

"No, it's not weird. I think if I went to your country, the same thing would happen to me. It's called culture; we are all different." Her cousin told her very kindly.

Aura finally dared to take a piece of food and taste it, she did it with the one that seemed the strangest to her, expecting to find a bitter taste, but she opened her eyes and said:

"This tastes very good."

"Everything is delicious. Give yourself a chance to enjoy it."

She continued tasting other foods, the meat, the other vegetables, some she knew, and she felt that each one had a new flavor, and although one or another she didn't like so much, she still ate it; her mother had taught her not to leave anything on the plate.

Her aunt, along with her cousin, were the ones who had gone to pick her up at the airport. Her uncle had not gone because he was working, and they did not know each other, so there was a lot of expectation for how that first meeting would be. Aura went by asking what he was like if he seemed in a good mood, if he was someone affectionate.

Her cousin, who was fond of making jokes, told her that he was sullen, that he would get angry for nothing, and then told her the truth, that he was not, that he was loving and very playful.

As Aura had so many things on her mind, anything could happen, and she was afraid.

As time went by, she played with her cousin and talked to her parents by video call. In her country, it was already night, and where she was at that moment, there was still a very bright sun. That also seemed curious to her, as she had always heard that it did not get dark at the same time all over the world due to the movement of the planet, but living it was a totally different experience.

Finally, her uncle arrived, walked through the door, and stood looking at her.

"This is a lovely girl." Said the uncle, opening his arms and pulling her in to greet her.

Her uncle was a thin man dressed in a suit and had a big mustache covering his upper lip.

"Hello, uncle," she said as she ran to greet him.

He picked her up and pressed her against his chest as he planted a kiss on her cheek.

He spoke the same language as Aura, but sounded a bit different. She thought it was funny how he talked, but didn't say anything.

Long before coming on this trip, Aura had seen that her aunt wore different clothes from her own. She noticed several pictures, and she especially liked the one with the purple and pink suit. It was beautiful and colorful. She had never seen anything like it, and she asked her mother why they dressed like that.

"It's the way they dress in their country. Don't you like it?" her mother said.

"Yes, I like these dresses, although I don't like my uncle's shirt. I think it's too flashy. Dad wears shirts with one color."

The mother laughed and told her they were a bit showy, but that's how they wore them there.

Now, in her uncle's and cousin's country, she stood before her aunt, who had a beautiful suit with gold lace and other flashy shades all over her garment, and her uncle, who, although dressed smartly, had a flashy shirt underneath.

"In your country, what games do you like to play?" Her uncle asked.

"I play soccer a lot. I have some friends in my area where we have a lot of fun. I love it." She said.

"I see. Do you want to play?" asked her uncle

Aura agreed immediately.

The three of them went out to the backyard of the house, from somewhere they took out a big ball, like the professionals, and began to play, without any rules of the sport, simply playing to take it away from each other and scoring in a goal that served as a target.

They had a lot of fun in their games. They spent at least an hour until the uncle, already sweaty and tired, sat down and asked for a break.

"Go on, children, this old man can't go on any longer," he said.

The two children laughed and continued playing; this time, one shot, and the other tried to catch the ball.

When they were both tired too, they went into the house. The cousin's mother appeared with some brightly colored drinks that she said were from local fruit. For Aura, again, it was a challenge. Still, she remembered that her mother had told her that she had to try new things in that country and that whatever they gave her, even though she didn't know it, it would be a unique experience. She couldn't refuse it without trying it first.

She held her breath, took the first sip, and tasted it. She was surprised. It was sweet, she could not describe it, but it was like a mixture of watermelon for its refreshing, banana for its creaminess, and peach for its consistency. But it was more, it was as if she had mixed many fruits. She asked her aunt, but she said no, it was only one fruit, and that she would show it to her later.

"We have a present for you," said her uncle.

He motioned to his cousin's mother, and she went off into one of the rooms and soon after returned with a box that was wrapped in wrapping paper. If Aura had seen flashy things so far, this was the most attractive of all, very colorful that, if you put them against the sun, would illuminate a whole street.

She began to uncover the gift, which had a red ribbon with a beautiful bow on top. It was light, and she could not imagine what it could be. She unwrapped it while her uncle, aunt, and cousin watched expectantly for her reaction.

When she uncovered it, she found something that lit up her face. It was a finely folded piece of cloth. She touched it. It was very soft. It could almost slide through her fingers.

She took it out. It was a pink dress with golden lace at the corners of the sleeves and neck. She knew immediately that it would fit her perfectly as if she had been measured.

"Your mother told us that you liked some of my dresses," said her aunt.

Aura nodded.

"Our tailor-made one with the measurements your mother sent."

Aura remembered that weeks ago her mother had been going through a lot of her clothes, she knew she was preparing the surprise at that moment, she made a mental note that she would congratulate her.

She spent the vacation season learning new things, open to enjoying every experience, and dressed as if she were just another local. She knew that giving herself the opportunity to learn about other cultures and respecting them was the way to nurture her experiences.

♥

If you dare to enjoy each new culture, venture into worlds you have not seen before, respecting what each one has. You will enter a universe where you will come out more prepared and know that the world is different and rich in customs.

The Writer

Have you started chasing dreams and feel like they're too far away? Do you want to achieve something, and it doesn't work out the first time? You may not know it, but in order to achieve dreams, you have to work to achieve them. Patience is important and is the cornerstone.

Lori always dreamed of being a famous writer, even when she was very little. She wanted people to read the stories she thought of, stories that took her to magical places. She loved reading and writing, and when she was a little girl, she quickly read any book she got.

She had written some short stories and poems to her pets, her parents, and her grandmother. What she loved most was her collection of short stories that together made a great story.

Every day she saw her writings, she felt very happy. She was inspired and invented a new story.

One day she wanted to participate in a joint reading of great writers of the city. She wanted to be an inspiration for other children.

She asked her mother if she could participate and if she would buy her more notebooks and pencils.

Her mother told her that as soon as she left, she would go to the stationery store to get everything she had asked for.

Her mother showed up with a ream of paper and several notebooks, as well as many colored pencils. That day was one of the happiest. She went to her room and set up a small studio where she spent hours writing and thinking up stories. Although she had this studio now, deep down she felt she could write even better. Change verbs, eliminate adjectives, put more poetry in some sentences, and change outcomes.

She asked herself many questions about how to make her work better.

"If I want to be a famous writer, I have to learn how to be one."

She found a creative writing class at the local library and signed up to improve her writing. She saw that she was making many mistakes and worked to improve them. Over the next few days, she felt that her writing was getting better and better.

When she felt confident enough, she went to a literary café where the most famous writers of the city were present and wanted to apply to do a reading for everyone.

The woman who was attending smiled sweetly when she saw her:

"Thank you for visiting us, but sadly we are not accepting new writers now. Maybe you can come next year because we already have a full schedule."

Lori felt very sad, but this did nothing but push her to keep preparing. She went to more classes and worked. She even got more praise for her writing, and those who read her were overwhelmed by her solid stories and unforgettable characters.

The next year, Lori brought more of her stories to show. The same lady from last year was there. When the lady saw Lori's new stories, she looked surprised. She could see Lori's writing had gotten better, but she still said no.

Lori was so sad. "Don't you like my stories?" she asked.

The lady replied, "Your stories are really good, Lori. But I think you can do even better if you keep practicing. I can't say yes this time."

Lori went home disappointed, sat down in the living room, and looked at all the books she had been accumulating for years. She had been working on becoming a better writer for some time. She remembered each of the classes she had taken and remembered a pattern in everything.

Many writers she learned about had to write for a long time before people noticed them. She read about famous writers and found out that many of them got told 'no' a lot before they became famous.

Lori felt a little better and started writing again. She worked hard and started writing a special series of stories from her heart. The words felt even more magical than before.

Just as she was finishing her story on the computer, Lori accidentally deleted a really important chapter.

"Oh no!" she exclaimed, feeling really sad.

She tried everything to get it back and even asked a computer expert for help. But he said it was gone for good. Now her story was missing a big piece, the part that made the story exciting, not the thoughtful or poetic parts. Tears filled Lori's eyes. After all her hard work, she had lost one of her favorite chapters.

Feeling upset, Lori went back to the computer to try and fix her story. The next day, as she read it all over again, including the part where the chapter was missing, she noticed something special. Even without that chapter, readers could use their imagination to fill in the blanks. This made her story even more unique and left people thinking. She realized that sometimes, mistakes can lead to new ideas.

When it was time to go to the famous literary café to

knock on the door again, she did not feel so sure. She wasn't confident because she expected the woman to reject her again.

"Nice to see you again," the lady said when she saw Lori walk in. "Every year you bring something new. I'm excited to see what you have this time!"

"This year, I didn't want to bring loose writings or snippets of stories, but I was encouraged to bring a composition that was accidentally interesting."

"Well, let's read it, then."

Lori handed her the book, and the lady said she needed some time to read it carefully. Lori nodded and started looking at other books in the store. As the woman read, she was pulled into the stories. There were surprising twists, deep thoughts sprinkled throughout, and lines that read like poetry. It was clear that a lot of love and hard work had gone into writing it.

Lori's heart felt like it was dancing in her chest. She had finally made it! That night, she and her parents went out for a special dinner. Lori could hardly wait for the day she'd read her stories at the café and meet other writers. "We are very proud of you," said her parents.

"Are you proud because I wrote something good?"

"Yes, but more so because you didn't give up despite rejections. You always stood up. You could have given up at any time, even with trouble on the way, but you showed love and patience, and now you have here the prize for the effort."

She went home happy that day and would soon enjoy a full house reading with people in awe of a young woman with such writing gifts.

On the day of her reading, Lori felt a mix of nerves and excitement. As she finished her last sentence, she looked up and saw everyone's faces. They looked touched by her words. And then, to her surprise, everyone stood up and started clapping. She had seen applause before, but this felt different. It wasn't just polite clapping - they were really cheering for her. Lori felt tears in her eyes. They weren't just being nice; they truly loved her story.

You should never give up on your dreams, even if many obstacles appear along the way. Lori didn't.

It may take longer than expected to achieve your dreams, but you can get what you want, so don't be discouraged by the obstacles you encounter along the way. Keep building your craft, and soon you will be the best writer, painter, or whatever you want to be.

The Light-up Skates

Have you ever wanted something so much that you might do something silly? Have you ever had the chance to keep something and return it? In this story, you'll get to know about a girl who desired a pair of skates with all her heart.

Danielle didn't want to go, but her mother said she couldn't stay home alone, so they had to go to the supermarket because they had nothing in the pantry. While they were in the store, in an area next to the technology section, she found something that immediately caught her attention. It was the sports section, and on one of the shelves were some incredible skates, beautiful, unlike any she had ever seen. The wheels lit up. They were black as the night and had rainbow-colored laces.

From that day on, all she could think about were the skates. It was love at first sight.

Danielle loved those skates so much that she drew pictures of herself skating in them all over town.

After school, whenever she was nearby with her mom, she'd look at those skates in the window.

"I want those skates, Mom," she told her.

"They are pretty," her mom replied.

"I see why you like them."

One day, her little brother came along and said, "Don't you already have skates at home?"

"They're old and one of the wheels is wobbly," Danielle explained.

"But they still work," her brother pointed out. Danielle didn't say anything but gave her brother a dirty look.

"I wish for those skates even if Mom thinks I don't need them and even though my brother says I have some already."

A week flew by, and when Danielle looked at the display, her beloved skates were gone, replaced by a soccer ball.

"Where are my skates?" Danielle said, a little anxious.

"At our home, in the storeroom where you left them.", her brother said.

"Not those, shush!" Instead, Danielle said, "those from the store".

"They probably sold them." Her mother said.

"I wanted them."

"I'm sorry, these things happen".

Now she felt very sad, thinking she would never be happy.

A few days later, on her way home, Danielle spotted a pair of skates at the park, identical to the ones from the store.

"Who left these skates here?" Danielle wondered aloud, feeling as if they were meant for her. Seeing no one around, and noticing the matching skate nearby, Danielle felt like the universe had given her a gift. Unable to resist the temptation, she picked them up and hurried home, her heart full of excitement.

When she got home, Danielle quickly stashed the skates in the storeroom, making sure they were well-hidden. She decided to keep them there until she could talk to her parents about them. Each day, whenever she got a chance, she sneaked a peek at the gleaming skates, her feelings a mix of joy and guilt.

That guilt grew every time she thought about the skates. Something about having them just didn't feel right.

One day at school, she unintentionally overheard two girls talking.

"Did you hear what happened to Lara?"

"No, what?"

"She lost her new skates. She left them in the park

near her house, and they weren't there when she returned".

"I can't believe it; I always told her not to leave them around; they were so pretty, and someone could steal them".

"Yeah, poor thing, they were a birthday present. When she came back, there was nothing there".

"I would never leave such beautiful skates alone. She didn't deserve this. She must be devastated".

After class, many students gathered at the park to help Lara search for her missing skates. Despite their efforts, the skates were nowhere to be found. Lara was devastated. She shared how her father had worked overtime just to buy those skates for her birthday. Now, due to her carelessness, they were gone.

The whole day, Danielle felt a heavy weight on her heart, knowing she had Lara's skates. The weight of guilt made her so exhausted that all she wanted to do was crawl into bed.

Lying down, her mind raced, thinking about how she

could right the wrong she had done.

"I didn't hear you", her mother said behind her, and Danielle jumped in fright.

"Are you okay? Why are you like this, with your eyes shining like you had cried?"

Her mother took the drawing and looked at it closely.

"Are you still sad about those roller skates we didn't buy you?"

"Kind of, but it's not what you think".

Danielle sighed and told her everything. When she finished, her mother said:

"You must return those roller skates to that girl; she must be very sad".

"Yes, I have to return the roller skates".

Her mother hugged Danielle tightly and kissed her forehead.

"You're doing the right thing".

"I know where Lara lives. I know her mom, so it's time to return those roller skates".

When they arrived at the house, Danielle told them how she had found the roller skates at the park and picked them up.

Lara's father smiled with great joy and said:

"Thank you, we were hoping they would turn up because Lara was very sad about them. Thank you for returning them".

As Danielle headed home, a smile spread across her face. Despite the past mistakes, she felt a warmth in her heart. The gnawing guilt that had upset her stomach for days had vanished. She realized that doing the right thing had brought her immense joy.

Her chest swelled with pride, knowing she had made the right choice. Her mother, while not saying a word, had a radiant smile that said it all. It was clear she was incredibly proud of her daughter's decision.

Always return things you find, even if you really want them. It's the right thing to do.

Opportunity to Win

Have you had the opportunity to cheat? Have you done it? Do you think it's okay to do so? This story is about how an opportunity may not be the best if your conscience has a price.

♥

Lisa doesn't think she's the bravest girl ever. For instance, if she sees a snake, she'd rather run away because she knows it's best to stay away from them. She hasn't ever fought a lion and she's even cautious around other people's dogs. However, she's faced tough challenges, like standing up to girls on her soccer team. She handled it so maturely, making her parents and family really proud.

During the soccer season, Lisa's team, The Reds, played lots of matches. They worked hard and made it all the way to the semifinals, hoping to win the championship. They had trained all year for this big moment.

Last season, The Reds had an amazing comeback during the playoff final. The whole crowd jumped to their feet, cheering loudly. It was one of the most memorable games that field had ever seen.

This season was tougher. Lisa and her team faced challenges and ended up winning fewer games than they lost, ranking them sixth out of eight teams.

In the next match, The Reds faced the White team, known for their powerful kicks and ranked third. Everyone was nervous, knowing the White team was tough and wanted to make it to the finals as much as The Reds did.

But The Reds came out strong, scoring the first goal

and keeping up the pressure. They had a plan to play offensively, with their forwards leading the charge and making sure the White team couldn't get close to their goal. Their strategy paid off, as The Reds scored two more goals than the White team, moving them forward to the next round.

The next weekend was a big one - it was the semifinals, and they were up against the Yellow team. Lisa was known for her powerful, muscular legs and her strong kicks. But the Yellow team had a player just like Lisa. This girl had strong legs too and was incredibly skilled at stealing the ball and driving it forward.

As the game progressed, Lisa spotted this girl, who was tall, almost as tall as her dad, charging towards the goal with speed and power. Despite Lisa's best efforts, she couldn't stop her. The girl took a powerful shot. It would've surely been a goal if their amazing goalkeeper hadn't made a fantastic save.

Lisa was frozen in place, her foot poised but without the ball, almost like a dancer in a ballet pose. She felt helpless, having already lost control of the ball.

Things seemed to go downhill from there. The Yellows played as if they had secretly watched and learned all of The Reds' strategies. They attacked fiercely and without pause. It felt to Lisa as though they were playing on ice, slipping and unable to keep up with the Yellows. In the end, The Reds lost by 3 goals.

But all hope wasn't lost. They still had one more chance to claim the third-place spot and bring home a trophy.

The next week, Lisa and her teammates got to the field early. They were set to play against familiar faces – some players they'd competed alongside in previous seasons, and even a coach they'd known for years.

The field was quiet, with the only sound being the collective breaths of the girls as they warmed up and readied themselves for the match. Before they knew it, the referee's whistle signaled the start of the game.

The opposing team was quick off the mark, pushing aggressively for the first goal – and they succeeded. As the scoreboard changed, Lisa felt a pang of disappointment. They had hoped that their lucky uniforms would give them an edge, but it seemed that luck wasn't on their side that day. They were down by one goal and the clock was ticking. Every second counted if they hoped to either level the score or edge ahead. Then, a glimmer of opportunity appeared when the ball went out of play.

"It's the Reds' turn to throw in the ball", said the referee.

The referee seemed confused about which team had the right to the throw-in. As a player from Lisa's team prepared to make the throw, Lisa caught a crucial detail – it was the other team that had last touched the ball, not The Reds. This meant that they weren't entitled to the throw-in. Lisa faced a dilemma. The Reds had a burning desire to win, and if they proceeded with the throw, they might have a chance to even the score or take the lead. But if the Whites got the throw and scored, they'd likely win the game.

Lisa's sense of fairness wrestled with her desire to win. If she stayed silent, they could potentially secure a victory. But would it be a victory worth having if it came at the cost of integrity?

Lisa nodded slowly, understanding what her coach meant. It wasn't about winning or losing; it was about doing the right thing even when it was hard.

"I wanted us to win," Lisa admitted, her voice quivering. "But I wanted to win the right way."

The coach put a comforting hand on Lisa's shoulder.

"That's what true sportsmanship is about. It's not just about the score on the board, but the choices you make on and off the field. Remember that, and you'll always be a winner in my eyes."

Lisa smiled, her heart full. She had learned a lesson more valuable than any trophy – the importance of honesty and integrity.

Lisa's words were simple but carried profound wisdom. Her teammates, coaches, and even some of the spectators could feel the weight of her decision. The field was silent for a moment, but the truth in Lisa's words rang out.

One by one, some of her teammates approached her. While some were still disappointed by the loss, others expressed their gratitude for Lisa's honesty and integrity. The younger players looked up to her, now seeing her not just as a talented soccer player but as a role model.

Even in the face of disappointment, Lisa had shown that winning isn't everything. The respect and trust of her peers were more valuable than any trophy.

Through her actions, she taught everyone present a valuable lesson about the importance of honesty and the true meaning of sportsmanship.

Hope, A Ray of Light

Have you ever seen those ads where people collect money for a sick person? Did you know that when you give, it helps them a lot? Would you like to help someone like that? Let's read about Camile. She kindly shared her light to help a sick person she didn't even know.

Camile arrived at her class with a purple bracelet with a large message written in eye-catching letters that said "Hope." All her friends started asking her what it was about, and she said it was to help people in need and that she had donated some money, and that's why she was wearing it.

It was a stretchy bracelet that had "Hope" on it. People got one when they gave money to help someone sick get medicine and tests. Since these things can cost a lot, the bracelets helped collect money.

Camile said it was for a friend's relative in another city who needed medical treatment. They needed to raise money for it.

The whole class was interested in what Camile was wearing, and she was very willing to tell them everything. She said that thanks to information brought by an uncle, someone was looking to raise money to undergo some tests and buy some medicines. The bracelets were designed exclusively to raise the necessary funds for medicines and whatever else was needed.

Camile noticed her friends were really interested. She thought they could not only sell bracelets but also do fun things like soccer games and camping to raise money. Her friends listened closely and wondered how much money they needed to help out.

After the conversation, finally, one of the boys said:

"I want one of those bracelets, and my mom will surely want to buy one too. How do we get them?"

"I want one too," said another.

Everyone wanted to buy a bracelet, eager to help and carry 'Hope' in their hearts.

A quiet girl in the class also said she'd get one, and hands shot up everywhere, showing everyone wanted to be a part of "Hope."

"I want one too," said another boy, known to be the kindest in the class. Everyone knew he came from a modest home. "I've got some savings; I hope it's enough."

Very quickly, many kids wanted bracelets. Camile started writing down names and collecting the money. She told everyone she'd bring the bracelets to school the next day.

The next day, everyone was excited and proud when Camile said they had raised a lot of money because so many people wanted bracelets, even outside of their classroom. They needed to get more bracelets because so many people wanted them! Just like the day before, many students said their families wanted bracelets too. Some asked for two, some for three, and one kid even asked for ten because all his cousins wanted one!

"Can we help in another way, like having a fair or preparing meals?" Everyone contributed ideas to see how they could gather more and more money for the sick person.

Everyone understood they couldn't have the fair at school or in the schoolyard. But they knew they could plan something fun outside of school. So, they started thinking of a plan together.

They went to the principal and asked if they could have a reading marathon to raise money for the sick person. The idea was that for one week, everyone would read as many pages as they could. They'd ask family and friends to give a little money for every page they read. By the end of the week, they hoped to have a lot of money to help out.

At the end of the week, every student brought in the money they raised from reading. They put all the money together for the sick person's care. Everyone was so happy because they were getting closer to their goal.

Other readers, even outside the school, wanted to help too. Some read a few pages each day, while others read really big books all at once. Every day after lunch, the teacher reminded the class to read a bit more. They dived into lots of fun stories. And remember, each word they read helped raise a little more money. They loved reading their books and felt proud when they finished.

"Hope" was an act of goodwill that started with Camile, who selflessly wore the bracelet and, when asked, told everyone what it was about. Thanks to that, many joined in and motivated others.

The money they raised was enough to help that person get back on their feet.

Later, they received a thank-you note, especially for Camile's beautiful heart.

If we can help others, it's a kind thing to do.

Orthodontics

Have you ever had braces, retainers, or something that makes you look different? Do you feel self-conscious about it? This is the story of a girl who is afraid of what her classmates will say when they see her with braces and who ultimately learns a great lesson for herself.

Many thoughts were running through Camile's mind that day, but what worried her the most was how her classmates would react when they saw her with this new appearance. What would they say when they saw her now and for a long time? She didn't know exactly what to expect, but she was certain that it would be different from when they saw her for the first time years ago when she had no braces or dental equipment. Today, standing in front of the school she had entered so many times before, she didn't want to leave the car and walk through the door.

From the back seat, she looked out the window and saw other kids standing by the school entrance. A funny feeling bubbled up from her tummy, making her feel a little sick. Taking a deep breath to hold back tears, she slowly opened the car door and stepped out, even though her feet felt really heavy. She felt so self-conscious, like everyone could see the wires on her teeth. It seemed hard to close her mouth right, and she thought people would only see her braces and not her. Then, her mom waved goodbye and drove off. She was on her own now, and she had to be brave.

Now at the school, Camile felt really alone, like she was lost in a big forest. As she walked, she didn't see any friends from last year. She was in a new grade, and sometimes kids got mixed into different classes. Her dad always told her first impressions were important, and she worried about what the new kids would think of her braces. Her old friends knew she needed them to straighten her teeth. But the braces had black bands on them, so when she smiled, her white teeth looked like they had black stripes. She felt a bit self-conscious about that.

Many kids were waiting near the closed doors. Camile felt like they were all looking at her, even if she didn't meet their eyes. She kept her mouth shut but still felt they were curious about her braces. She kind of understood why they might be staring. In her mind, with her tiny braces and teeth getting straighter, she felt she must look really different.

Feeling a little upset, Camile thought of asking the kids, "Why are you staring?" But then she decided it was best to just ignore them. She turned away and sat on a bench, looking at a tree. She felt like crying and quickly wiped away a tear.

She looked down at her uniform. It was neat and smelled freshly ironed. It felt soft and pretty. Yet, she felt like crying. She thought that no matter how nice she dressed, people would just see her braces. She felt trapped. She couldn't enjoy ice cream or crunchy snacks and had to brush her braces all the time.

At first, the braces pinched her lips and it was uncomfortable. But she got used to that feeling. What she really didn't like was everyone seeing her black braces against her white teeth. The doctor said black was a strong color for braces. But Camile wished they were fun rainbow colors instead.

While looking at the tree, she felt a tingling in her neck. She felt like she was being looked at without disguise. She didn't want to meet those curious people who couldn't stop looking at her. She thought she should be used to that kind of gaze by now.

She felt out of place, different from the other kids with straight teeth, or even those with gaps from lost baby teeth. She couldn't hide her braces when she spoke. Every time she opened her mouth, her metal-covered teeth would be on display. Some kids could talk without showing their teeth, but not Camile. Every time she spoke, her braces were the center of attention.

Sweat trickled down her back and arms. On top of feeling self-conscious about her braces, she now felt sweaty, imagining she might smell like how her older brother did after his soccer games.

But that day, she could overcome it; despite those

ugly thoughts, she managed to make friends, and everyone got used to seeing her teeth like that, in fact, they didn't even say anything.

Time passed, and many appointments where the doctor squeezed and adjusted her teeth with a machine, and the date of that treatment ended, it was time for them to come off. That day Camile was so happy that she hugged the doctor and said she had regained her freedom.

When she left there, she wanted to call Alicia, her best friend, to tell her what had happened, but she wanted to surprise her the next day instead. She had a strong desire to hear everyone's admiration when she smiled with her white and aligned teeth, without strange braces on them. She wouldn't have to go with that ugly thing anymore; she felt her mouth was liberated. So that morning, while there, she waited for the others.

Although Camile smiled more than usual, no one commented anything in the first class. She didn't understand what was happening. She had looked at herself in the mirror for hours and felt like she had the most beautiful smile in the world. She thought maybe everyone was worried because it was a math class, and they didn't notice, but they would in the next class. But again, she waited, and nothing happened. After a while, she felt bad. She thought she would be ugly with or without braces because no one noticed. At the end of the day, she was very upset that no one, not even Alicia, her best friend, had said anything. She hated wearing braces in her mouth.

Perhaps she was just as ugly without the braces, or maybe her friends didn't care about her as much as she thought. Finally, seeing Alicia, she said:

"Do you see anything different about me?"

"Did you cut your hair?"

"No, it's not my hair."

"Did you paint your nails with glitter?"

"No."

"I don't know."

"It's my braces; they're gone!"

Camile smiled at her with all her big, white teeth.

Alicia looked at her, unconcerned, and said, "Oh, normal. I thought it was something extraordinary. It's fine. You looked fine with them, and you look fine without them"

Camile was upset, but that night, thinking about what had happened, she realized that her friends had not paid much attention to her braces. She had made a big deal of it herself, which is why they didn't even notice when she took them off.

Don't feel self-conscious about any limitations or having something on your body. Those who love you will accept you just the way you are, as wonderful as you show yourself every day.

Attention in Class

Do you sometimes feel like your wings are clipped? Do you have a great talent, but no one believes in you? This is the story of a girl who seems to have a difficult relationship with her teacher, but in the end, she finds herself and discovers what she is meant to be.

Zoey felt that school just wasn't the right fit for her. Since she started, she didn't feel good studying there, as if it wasn't her world. She didn't like her classmates, and many things bothered her. She didn't like the food they gave her, nor being near the window where the sunlight reflected off her notebook. She didn't like recess either because there was no room on the swings, and the kids ran around a lot, sometimes accidentally pushing her. But what she liked the least was her teacher, Nelly, who always seemed angry and didn't address her in the best way.

She had a certain behavior towards Zoey that made her feel different, as she never invited her to participate in some group activities, nor had she asked her to erase the blackboard or recite a lesson in front of the class. Although she asked her to sit in the front because she couldn't see the blackboard well, it seemed she wasn't paying attention. Although the same behavior could be seen with other children, the teacher seemed to overlook these things. For example, one day, she made Zoey sit behind Luis, the biggest kid in the class, so she had a hard time seeing the front since she only saw the large back of her classmate.

What the teacher Nelly did have were rules, even for going to the bathroom. She said they had to wait for her to be quiet and then raise their hand to ask for permission to leave, and if they could, they would go, or if not, they would go during recess.

One day the teacher announced:

"Today, you will take a sheet of paper and start writing. I want you to design a story about something that you found very interesting. I don't want repeated themes, so everyone's creativity has to be good."

She asked them to clear their desks so that each could write down their information without obstacles.

"Can we write about the amusement park in the city?" Laura asked.

"Yes, that would be perfect, but no one else should talk about that topic, even if they've been to that place."

Zoey opened the notebook where they usually wrote about those topics and tried not to pay attention to the big red "F" that said Deficient, must improve, which her teacher had given her on one occasion. Although she had done the same to half of the class.

The story she had written was about a family trip to

the beach, where she narrated the trip, how they had an accident on the way and almost hit a deer that was in the middle of the road. The teacher then told her it was too much imagination and that stories should stick to facts, not fiction. She didn't believe her, no matter how much Zoey insisted it was real.

Zoey accepted that her teacher gave her an "F" grade because she had corrected her writing, style, and spelling. Still, she could not tolerate her questioning her truth. It was an important trip, and what she experienced she remembered vividly: the deer's fur almost on the car, the parents screaming, and then how they carefully drove past it the road even though it didn't move and had to wait a while for it to want to move forward.

Teacher Nelly wrote the guidelines to follow for designing the story. First, it had to be about something new and non-fiction. It had to be told in three paragraphs of detail, one to conclude and one to start, and one where everything was summarized, but without revealing key details of the story, just to hook the reader.

Laura had her notebook with good grades, and the teacher seemed to validate everything for her but not for the others. On the other hand, Zoey and her classmates had "F" grades in all their notebooks and hateful notes from the teacher.

Zoey began to see a hole in the classroom wall, which seemed to lead to a cave at the top of a mountain that seemed to descend into the mouth of the earth's center. There were two nail holes on the sides, which were small alternative paths.

She looked around, and the brick ceiling of the wall where the hole was, was the plateau where the cave was. She saw animals, a giant bear roaring, and birds flying and cawing suspiciously. The dirty glass window was the clouds gathering about to burst into a torrential downpour. Zoey, seeing all this, thought she could make another story, this time telling something completely fictional, opposing the teacher's idea, and setting aside the family stories she never believed.

Zoey opened her notebook and started writing, letting her creativity take over, creating landscapes, situations, and all kinds of characters.

She finished the task and handed in her notebook for the teacher to correct. Days later, the teacher placed the notebooks on each seat. Zoey opened hers and found her story, "The cave in the wall." She felt very excited and went to the bottom, looking for the grade. Instead, in a red that seemed redder than ever, it said "F" and a message, "What a fantastical and false story."

Zoey felt angry and wanted to say something, but she only limited herself to wiping away the tears that burned her.

She noticed her notebook had tear stains. She must have cried a lot without even realizing. With a huff, she quickly closed her notebook, and the sound echoed in the classroom. Teacher Nelly glanced at her, looking over her glasses. She didn't say anything but had a little smile, like she was happy to see Zoey upset. Later, during recess, Zoey was on a bench, tears still in her eyes. After some time, she heard Laura's voice behind her:

"Hello," she said, "I think the teacher didn't grade you well again."

"That's right."

"Well, class started minutes ago, and she asked me to come and get you."

Zoey didn't say anything, and after a moment, Laura shrugged and left. Finally, Zoey, thinking about the situation, said to herself:

"She'll see, teacher; she'll see how I'll shut her mouth one day and show her my talent."

She returned to her class but with her pride restored.

On that day at home, she decided to search online for writing contests for kids, and when she found one, she submitted her story about the cave. Imagine her surprise when weeks later, she was announced as the winner.

She knew then that she had a great talent for storytelling, and even though there would be teachers or people around her who would doubt her talent, she constantly prepared herself to be the best. She improved her spelling and writing skills, fueled her imagination, and never stopped reading, inspiring her to create her own worlds.

At that time, Zoey didn't know, but years later, she would become one of the most talented writers in the country. More than doing harm, teacher Nelly helped Zoey see herself, believe in herself, and take the step to confirm what she already knew she was, a talented writer.

Don't let anyone undermine who you are. If you have a talent and feel good about it, keep moving forward and improve every day.

Made in the USA
Las Vegas, NV
12 November 2024

11703963R00042